Endorsements for
Ten Practices of Effective Boards

A wise man once encouraged us to "go to the ant" to learn important truths about life. In much the same way, Ken Coley is encouraging us to "go to the dogs" to learn something important about governance in the Christian school. In a winsome, insightful parable in which canines serve as stand-ins for us mere mortals, Dr. Coley introduces and illustrates key principles and practices that make quality governance a real possibility. This is a highly readable book with important lessons for anyone in Christian school leadership.

—**Dr. Alan Pue**
President, The Barnabas Group, Colorado Springs, Colorado

These engaging and entertaining canine tales make the case for effective board governance. The ten specific and grace-filled practices are brilliant in their diagnosis and treatment of the board through proven principles of operational excellence. All board members should prayerfully and carefully read this book.

—**Dr. S. L. Sherrill**
Founder and Superintendent of North Raleigh Christian Academy, Raleigh, North Carolina

Ken Coley, in his inimitable style, has captured the essence of board governance. Though these practices make common sense, in reality they are far too uncommon in Christian schools. Ineffective boards, administrative turnover and burnout, and institutional mediocrity are the result. Quality schools are ultimately built on deferential relationships with board and administration knowing their proper roles and striving to maintain those relationships. *Do two walk together unless they have agreed to do so* (Amos 3:3)? This fable gets to the heart of what will make a school thrive. A few practices, lived out, can make all the difference.

—**Timothy Duff**
Headmaster of Pioneer Valley Christian School,
Springfield, Massachusetts

Well trained board members can be a wonderful blessing to a school but untrained ones can be a school's greatest liability. Using a canine parable Ken Coley offers essential instruction for anyone who wants to serve effectively on a Christian school board—and he does it in a thought provoking, entertaining and sometimes touching manner. The narrative is a first rate and memorable guide for board members that will ultimately benefit their Christian schools and their students!

—**Mark Kennedy**
Director ACSI Eastern Canada

TEN PRACTICES
OF
EFFECTIVE
BOARDS

TEN PRACTICES
OF
EFFECTIVE
BOARDS

A UNIQUE TALE ABOUT BOARD GOVERNANCE

KENNETH S. COLEY

HELMSMAN
BOOKS

NAVIGATING LEADING & TEACHING

HELMSMAN BOOKS

NAVIGATING LEADING & TEACHING

To order additional copies of this book
please visit our website at
www.helmsman.org

For information about having the author lead a seminar

contact him at kcoley@sebts.edu

ISBN 13: 978-1-63068-567-6
ISBN 10: 978-1-63068-569-0

DEDICATION

This book is dedicated to Dr. John Schimmer, Jr., a man who has dedicated his life and ministry to Christian schools. John has coached countless administrators and school boards around the world on multiple topics, including philosophy, strategic planning, and finances. He served as the director of the ACSI South-Central Regional Office from 1978-2004. Many leaders consider Dr. Schimmer's greatest contribution to be in the area of school governance. He is a published authority, and many school leaders like me are indebted to the precision of his thinking and the clarity of his writing. And we are all a lot wiser because of the "schimmerisms" that always made their way into his presentations.

CONTENTS

FOREWORD

I F A RECURRENT issue has plagued the Christian school movement for the past thirty years, it has been the lack of effective governance by trustees. School governance seems to be an inexact science in the public school sector and it appears to be worse, and perhaps more debilitating, in the Christian school. Often one or two trustees are elected or appointed to the board, and shortly afterward an administrator loses a position, and the school suffers. Unfortunately, personal agendas, petty politics, and power plays are common. Board governance and trustee conduct should serve as the model of Christian ethics and behavior for administrators, faculty members, school staff, parents, community, and most of all students.

A healthy respect for the position of trustee and a dedication to personal and corporate ethics is needed at the governance leadership level, by every board member. Trustee positional respect includes a reverence for the God they serve and a deep regard for the divine and eternal aspects of the influence that they wield across the organization. While there are several models of governance that are quite effective, the bottom line is the quality of the individuals who serve, the procedural boundaries they observe, and the relational ethics between them and the head of the school.

Dr. Ken Coley provides, in this insightful fable, the basis for any school board to engage in a healthy dialog about its governance model, ethics, policies, behavior, and their impact on the school they serve. The use of a variety of breeds of dog and their related gifts and behaviors is an enjoyable way to get at some of the issues boards face and engage in a dialog that is honest, healthy, educational, and inspirational. It also brings to mind the "body-life" (1 Cor. 12) principles that every effective board models for the school community.

Every trustee, and particularly anyone who has chaired a board or led the board, will identify quickly with the analogies of working with a varied pack. Dr. Coley captures the essential elements of the relationships that exist within organizational structures. He deals subtly with the emotional and passionate sides of power and authority in relationships and pointedly with the practical realities of how they apply to boardsmanship. The character requirements for effective board members include mutual submission, deference, regard, wisdom, and perseverance. These find their way into the various situations in the fable.

I had the personal and professional joy of serving on a school board for more than twenty years that modeled, mentored, and managed themselves and me with a gracious, forbearing spirit and much aplomb. Dr. Coley's worthy work on governance will be a help and a blessing to move more boards toward this type of effectiveness and stability. I heartily commend your diligent attention, thoughtful

FOREWORD

contemplation, lively discussion, and strong adherence to its principles.

—**Derek J. Keenan**, EdD
Association of Christian Schools International, Vice President,
Academic Affairs

INTRODUCTION

THIS BOOK HAS allowed me to spend time with two of my great loves: Christian school leadership and dogs, man's best friends. The former is my calling, the latter my hobby. The leadership part is messy and complex. The canine part is uncomplicated, straightforward, and even sublime. The two come together in this story, which has moved me to tears many times as I have revisited episodes of heartbreak that I have heard from many administrators and school leaders. From Canada to Haiti to Cuba and all the states in the U.S., many dedicated servants of God have expressed emotions of frustration, heartache, and even bitterness because of power and authority misused or abused. At the same time, I have looked into the deep, sensitive eyes of my German Shepherds and recognized their desire to be loved, respected, and properly trained. However, without "an understanding" between master and dog, the pet will rise up and take over the house.

But I must hasten to add that, frequently, the disconnect between administrator and board is not based on a carnal grab for power but merely a misunderstanding of how to do the basics of board governance. From this perspective I have narrowed the typical training manual to a succinct list of ten practices that lead to effective governance.

After reading this book, a board member should consider his participation in the life of his school and the opportunity for the entire board to have common ground for the meaningful discussion of vital tenets of effective school governance. Each chapter will examine one or more of these primary concepts by presenting them in the life of a group of neighborhood dogs who are motivated to establish a school so their puppies "learn to obey the Master." Each chapter can be discussed in isolation, though the story flows with an overall narrative. A series of questions and talking points at the end of each chapter will help move readers from considering the interaction of the story's characters to evaluating the dynamics of their own organization.

In presenting this book to leaders of school boards or non-profit boards, I recognize I am asking readers to consider a different approach to board training. With the potential for some reluctance on your part, I would like for you to consider the following quote from the foreword of *Our Iceberg Is Melting*: "Our method is showing, much more than telling, and showing with the method that has helped more people learn over the centuries than any other single technique: the fable.

"Fables can be powerful because they take serious, confusing, and threatening subjects and make them clear and approachable. Fables can be memorable, unlike so much of the information that bombards us today and is forgotten tomorrow. They can stimulate thought, teach important lessons, and motivate anyone—young or old—to use those lessons. In our modern, high-tech world, we can easily forget this simple yet profound truth" (pp. 3-4).

INTRODUCTION

As much as I love my characters, I was careful not to extend their thinking and conversation into the realm of spiritual discourse or create an imaginary connection to God or the Holy Spirit. In the appendix, "What Dogs Can't Do," I encourage the reader to consider what God's Word has to say about governance and proper relationships within the body of Christ. Each of these references would be ideal as a stand-alone passage for devotions when your board gathers for training or at its regular meeting.

Now I invite you take a leisurely walk through my neighborhood and meet some fascinating friends.

THE DREAM

BIG DOG, A humongous Saint Bernard, loved the little puppies in his neighborhood. He loved their energy, tiny yelps, constant chewing, playfulness, and best of all, their insatiable appetite to learn.

Tonight, though, a burden hung on his heart like a heavy dog collar. One of his favorites, Bandit, couldn't be found. The mischievous guy wasn't responding to the impatient calls of his masters. Big Dog wondered why Bandit hadn't learned the boundaries of his yard. And why would the little pup disregard all of his training?

Big Dog joined the search, not by invitation or out of obligation, but because Bandit had earned a special place in his heart. He couldn't bear the thought of his buddy being gone. Big Dog fought back tears.

He first searched the neighborhood playground that teemed with the delicious scents of ice cream and hot dogs. Big Dog then jogged the length of the main road in the neighborhood, a four-minute trot that covered about fifty homes. Still no Bandit. So Big Dog doubled back along a creek that bounded the development on one side.

Just after dark, Big Dog heard more whistling from Bandit's master. Each owner had a distinct tone, and it had become part of the nightly melody of the neighborhood. But tonight the whistling had a shrill tone to it. And the repeated call of "Bandit!" grew louder and more frantic.

Big Dog flopped down in his backyard, exhausted from running back and forth the last hour through the mile-long neighborhood. Everyone knew of his well-earned reputation as a Saint Bernard that had rescued many no matter the danger—deep forest, blowing snow, or driving rain. But tonight was different.

He could not find Bandit.

The one-year-old had earned his nickname honestly. Sneaking off with neighbors' tools or toys. Digging up lawns. Treeing cats. Late night howling. But never this—disappearing.

In the morning, if he had not returned, the rumors would begin: "His owner had had enough," "Bandit had gone too far," or "He had been spotted with a pack of wild dogs."

Someone else would say, "They caught a glimpse of him in the truck that belongs to the city."

And the worse one, "Bandit could be—"

Big Dog couldn't finish the thought. He sighed and collapsed into a deep sleep. He ran in place, digging a rut in the soft grass of his owner's home, and whined. Big Dog dreamed he was surrounded by young puppies who cried out for help. He scrambled to protect them, corral them, calm them, and discipline them. But there were too many and some slipped away into the darkness.

As Big Dog struggled to contain them, he became more and more agitated and his rotund body quivered as he tried

Big Dog

in vain to save all the puppies. Finally, he shook himself awake. Passing from deep sleep into consciousness, Big Dog contemplated the frustration of the previous night and the eerie dream that had stuck with him. A thought that lingered at the edge of his mind bullied its way to the front. He pondered the notion and committed himself to finding a solution to this situation. He made it a goal that the neighborhood would not lose another young dog on his watch. Still unsure of the final solution, Big Dog knew his actions might not bring back Bandit, but he wasn't about to lie around while other pups ran from their Masters.

A black and tan blur interrupted Big Dog's pensive trance. The blur's name was Jessie, a young German Shepherd with more energy than sense. She was conducting her morning reconnaissance of the neighborhood—chasing anything and everything that moved. Larger life forms got her attention first: birds, squirrels, rabbits, and other

Little Bandit

puppies. After failing to capture any of these intruders, Jessie turned her attention to butterflies, moths, and any insects moving in the grass. One need not be a trained educator to evaluate that this six-month-old was easily distracted.

Big Dog was transfixed by the puppy's playfulness, intensity, and energy. The comedic behavior of the young dog broke the spell of gloom that hung over him. Watching the little dog's industriousness was both entertaining and reassuring. She was spectacular in her confirmation and markings—long, muscular legs; sleek, glistening fur; huge, quick paws; and playful, intelligent eyes. Indeed, she was fearfully and wonderfully made.

Like a doting grandfather, Big Dog imagined what Jessie could become, given the right training. He thought if her power and potential could be harnessed, if she could be taught to obey the Master, and if she could learn self-discipline, then she would not become one of the disturbing little specters in his dream that slipped unnoticed into the dark of his imagination. Instead, this magnificent creation would fulfill her intended purpose and live a long, productive life.

How this would unfold was taking shape in his mind's eye. But take shape it would and the other adult canines would soon participate in his vision.

DISCUSSION:

> ➤ Are the needs of young families and children in your community reflected in the events and culture of Big Dog's neighborhood?
> ➤ Do these needs change over time?
> ➤ Has God inspired a group of concerned believers, such as a founding committee, to respond to a particular vision in response to these needs? What is our Master requiring of you in your community?

2

THE MISSION

A WEEK LATER, AS dusk settled over his neighborhood, Big Dog stepped to the door with a mixture of hope and anxiety. Would any other dogs join him or would he be forced to go this alone? And if others came, which ones? He kept a lonely vigil at the door for several minutes before the first arrivals.

They were full of questions and advice, but Big Dog shooed them into his spacious one-room house and encouraged them to find a place on the straw that covered the floor from corner to corner.

Soon after, a group that thought this was a social gathering paraded in, preening for the rest of the group as if they were being judged at a dog show. These were followed by the final group who rushed in late, acting as though this meeting was interrupting important business elsewhere.

After the last group entered, Big Dog took his place at the head of the room. Glancing around the now crowded room, Big Dog's fretfulness subsided. He realized there would be strength in numbers if all those gathered joined him in this adventure.

Nearest to Big Dog was Kelley, a friendly, energetic Cocker Spaniel, who was willing to try almost anything, as long as someone else came up with the idea. Next to Kelley sat her friend from down the street, Reneé, a French poodle, who appeared to have had her hair and nails done just for the occasion. Bright and opinionated, her participation would not go unnoticed.

Rusty, a reddish brown Lab, who smelled of anything to do with hunting and the back of an old pickup, nestled in close to Reneé. Closest to the door was Keta, a restless Husky who appeared to be ready to bolt at a moment's notice.

Renee

To Big Dog's left sat Winston, a British Bulldog, who was well known for being stubborn and belligerent. Wedged into a dark corner was Sage, a Shar Pei, who was the oldest in attendance and easily the quietest dog of the group.

Corky and Sport were the last two members in the circle. Corky was strikingly handsome, though no one could identify the various breeds from which his features came. Sport was a muscular dog that towered over all the others, with the exception of Big Dog.

Rusty

An impressive pack, Big Dog thought, intelligent, fierce, disciplined, diverse, and all known for being obedient to their Master.

Not surprisingly, Keta was the first to speak. "Why are we here? I have places to go!"

Rusty chimed in. "I'm going hunting before dawn and need to get some sleep."

Others joined in and the room quickly became chaotic, cramped, and smelly.

Big Dog cleared his throat in a manner that could have been mistaken for a growl. The room fell silent. He reminded them all of the frequency with which puppies were "lost," the recent tragedy of Bandit's disappearance, and the powerful dream he had had that fateful night.

"What I believe we need to do is establish a school that I suggest we call Canine Academy. Our pups can attend and we can see to it that we don't lose any more."

He pulled a sheet off the wall to reveal something he had written earlier in the day. His dark eyes were filled with compassion and intensity as he read what he hoped to accomplish:

Keta

Canine Academy: Training young dogs to obey their Master

Winston

Sage spoke first, his excitement evident. "This is exactly what our pups have needed! Many are in situations where they have no positive role models—"

"And in some homes the master is cruel or distant," Kelley said. "The pups don't have a chance to understand what is expected."

Rusty jumped into the discussion. "I wasn't born knowing how to hunt! Someone had to show me and train me. It took time; I wasn't the fastest learner."

"I always hated to be inside all day without a chance to be exploring," Keta

Sport

added. "A lot of dogs don't get the attention they need and opportunities to grow."

As other dogs started to speak on top of each other, Winston's gruff voice brought order. "Some pups have no clue that there are rules to follow for their own good. They need to learn to obey."

"If each dog can learn to obey his Master, then he can live at peace with the Master and learn to serve him, as it was intended to be," Sage said. The others nodded at his summarization.

Big Dog's heart pounded with excitement. "So we are all agreed. This is our vision for our puppies and the founding of Canine Academy."

Every representative howled his/her approval. The meeting ended and those in attendance agreed to gather again soon to make more plans. As they scattered, Big Dog sighed, circled his now-spacious house three times, and settled in for a long, peaceful rest.

DISCUSSION:

➢ What is your opinion of Big Dog's reason for beginning Canine Academy? Compare this concept with Scripture, such as Psalm 1:1-3.

➢ Do you recall the initial motivation to begin your school? Are that story and vision still alive?

➢ In what ways do the leaders introduce the vision and mission of the school to the new members of the community?

➢ How effective is your board in promoting the school in your community? Does every board member understand they must be an ambassador for the school to introduce the school to friends and acquaintances?

Sage

3

THE ADMINISTRATOR

HAVING REACHED AGREEMENT on the purpose of the school and the overall outcome it desired for their puppies, the Board turned its attention to finding a leader for the new school. The members realized that even though they had all been to school, that didn't make any of them qualified to run one. They also knew they didn't know a lot of details regarding how to go about it, but they knew this hire would be the most important. This leader would become the face of the school and have charge over the staff.

Big Dog printed this policy on the wall of their meeting place:

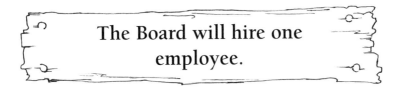

The Board will hire one employee.

TEN PRACTICES OF EFFECTIVE BOARDS

Over the course of many weeks, Big Dog listened to the members offer their opinions on how to hire the right person. One recommended a friend who was "a strong leader." Another asked to consider a friend who "has a lot of experience after raising twenty puppies!" Normally quiet, Sage offered the best suggestion. The Board wasted no time in heeding his advice: first develop a job description, including a list of qualifications.

Hashing out the qualifications was difficult, but the Board decided it could not hire a representative from the following breeds:

A pit bull—too fierce
A hunting breed—easily distracted by passing wildlife
A sled dog—prone to take a walk on the wild side
A lap dog—not motivated to do much

The Candidates

Serious consideration led to the conclusion that the Board needed some type of shepherd. These breeds have the reputation for being obedient to their Master. They can be loyal and are generally thought to be submissive to the will of the one in charge, which would be the Board in this case. In addition, a shepherd would be diligent to get to know and to nurture each student, a must for their school. And when a student strayed, a member of this breed would have the discernment and tenacity to go out and bring him back. With this modeling in place, this type of leader would train others to follow his example.

The Board also decided the face of the school must have behavior congruent with the school's vision statement. These qualities emerged in the discussion and quickly became part of the job description. The Administrator would:

Point the way
Model the mission of the school
Hire and oversee the faculty and the teaching/learning process
Measure the progress of the school
Allocate the school's limited resources

After chewing on what they sought—the job description and the necessary qualities of the Administrator—the council decided the top three breeds were a German Shepherd, a Border Collie, and an Old English Sheep Dog.

To avoid turning the selection process into the dog walk at the Canterbury Kennel Club Show, the Board determined to rank order their final three and interview just one candidate at a time, starting with their top choice. So it began with Duke, a German Shepherd. His references described him as hard-working and obedient. When called upon, Duke demonstrated the ability to be the Alpha leader of a group. As a part of their due diligence, the Board checked with the German Shepherd Rescue and Adoption Agency

Duke

to make sure Duke had maintained a stable home life. The Board found no mention of Duke ever being put up for adoption. No disappearances. No lost and found reports. Duke's record was clean.

During a thorough interview, Duke convinced the Board he was their dog. Unfortunately, after all of the impressive preparations that had been made for his hiring, left unsettled were the decisions regarding how he would be evaluated. Would they need to keep Duke on a short leash? And who would decide when the leash needed pulling? And at some point, history shows, that leash would need to be pulled.

DISCUSSION:

Consider these perspectives and discuss where your board stands on each:

- ➤ The Administrator is the most important hire.
- ➤ He/she becomes the "face of the school."
- ➤ The Board hires only one employee.

Review and discuss the process:

- ➤ Writing the job description prior to interviewing
- ➤ Agreeing on qualifications that eliminate some candidates
- ➤ Evaluating the five-point job description. Should any additions be made?

Make a list of check points that need to be a part of the process of conducting a background search on a candidate for a position of this importance.

4

OUT OF BOUNDS

THE ATMOSPHERE WAS different inside the Board's meeting room. The fun and anticipation were chased away by tension and uncertainty. Everyone was present except for Reneé and no one expected her to return if the gossip was true. All of the representatives had heard some version of the story but just what had happened at school the day before was still unclear.

Big Dog quietly slipped out and trotted over to his Master's house, hooked up the hose, and turned on the water spigot. This was a preemptive move in case any members got out of line and needed a cold shower to calm down.

Big Dog returned and waited outside the front door for Duke to arrive. When he did, the two entered the meeting room. Keta, Winston, and Rusty clamored to speak over each other about policies, protocols, and missing a morning run while three others sat listening.

Big Dog cleared his throat, the deep rumble creating the silence he wanted. "Thank you for coming on short notice," he said. "I'm sure you've all heard about the events at school yesterday."

With a slight hint of irritation, Keta said, "I, for one, want to know *all* the details."

"Of course," Big Dog said. "We'll begin by hearing Duke's side."

Sport, a shepherd like Duke, blurted, "Why should we believe his side? He only wants to keep his tail out of the crack."

"Duke hasn't given us a reason to not believe him," Big Dog said. "I feel we need to hear his side of the story first." Big Dog scanned the room. When no one else objected, he turned to Duke. "Please."

Duke stepped forward and stared over the heads of the Board members. Big Dog knew Duke was a little nervous. During the walk to the meeting, the young head administrator admitted he feared a rumbling might signal a disaster for his leadership. Big Dog encouraged Duke to avoid eye contact and to stand with confidence. Remember what they taught you in training, Big Dog said—"Don't fidget or pace."

The Administrator, who had earned Big Dog's trust and affection, straightened into his classic German Shepherd sitting posture, where he remained for some time, except for the occasional shifting of his weight from one front leg to the other. "As you may recall, yesterday was a beautiful warm day. Since we had to keep the pups inside all week, I took the lead and we went for a long walk that ended at the creek."

He paused for a moment because he was interrupted by moans, grumbles, and a growl or two. Corky even stood up and circled his seat three times before repositioning himself.

"It has been my experience," Duke continued, "that some pups never learned to swim properly. So I thought that it would be a good opportunity to teach them while the creek was higher than normal and the water was deep enough."

Kelley shrieked and almost swooned. "What if one of them had been swept away? Isn't there a big dam downstream?"

Winston, ever the stickler for following the rules, joined in. "I don't recall discussing anything about swimming when we reviewed what we are teaching these kids."

"Quiet down," Big Dog barked and he nodded for Duke to continue.

"I hear what you are saying, but I am a trained water safety instructor. I checked the stream carefully and posted staff along the banks. However, I didn't think about them getting muddy. I'm sorry." He shifted weight from one leg to another. "But we did have half the group perfect their paddle."

Rusty and Corky nodded. Apparently Winston wasn't done. "Where's Reneé? I heard she had something to say about this."

"Yes," Duke picked up the story line. "She met me at the curb when we returned. Reneé saw that Gigi was covered in mud and was very upset. She chewed on my ear all the way back to the yard and included a few threats about the council."

Big Dog imagined the little white ball of manicured hair all matted down with water and mud from the creek bed. He swallowed his laughter. The pup probably had the time of her life.

"I understand you walked away," someone in the back said.

Having heard enough, Big Dog stepped in and wrote on the wall:

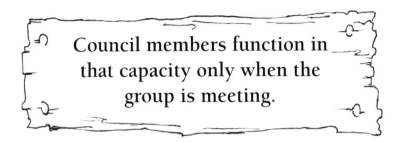

Council members function in that capacity only when the group is meeting.

"She was out of line for fussing at Duke in that manner," Big Dog said. "She was upset and overreacted. Duke and I will try to repair this relationship. But each of us has to understand that we don't have any authority apart from the decisions that we make as a group. "

Winston harrumphed his last complaint, "And one other thing, everyone knows that the creek is off limits. If Duke had stayed in the neighborhood, none of this would have happened."

Sage spoke first, which was good, because Big Dog didn't have a response.

"Has anyone told our Head of Academy that the creek is out of bounds?"

While the council considered its failure to adequately communicate, Big Dog added to the list of rules that the council needed to follow:

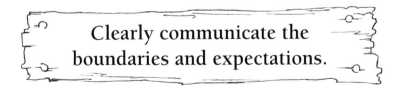

Clearly communicate the boundaries and expectations.

"Just because one or two or many of us think that it is obvious to everyone doesn't mean that the Administrator and teachers understand routines and procedures. We all have to work together to develop the policies that we want our Administrator to carry out." Again it seemed Sage was the voice of wisdom and discernment.

One downside of the "mud creek" event was Reneé's resignation, but because of her behavior the Board accepted it and moved on.

After the council went home, Big Dog trotted out and turned off the spigot. He chuckled to himself, relieved that he had not needed to turn the hose on anyone that night. A major league brawl had been avoided and the Board continued to grow.

DISCUSSION:

➢ What was the issue/conflict that made this meeting necessary?
➢ What is your evaluation of how Big Dog dealt with this conflict? And Duke?
➢ Evaluate how the Board in general went about ironing out the issues that were discussed in this chapter.
➢ Thinking back to the title, who was "out of bounds"?
➢ What are some potential pitfalls that you could foresee new staff or new administrators not understanding? (For example: The teaching of sex education or the proper handling of Creation versus Evolution.)
➢ What Scripture comes to mind that assists us in working through situations like the one presented here?

OUT OF BOUNDS

Review your board's procedures for the following:

> ➤ Handling conflict
> ➤ The Administrator's interaction at meetings
> ➤ Board's communication of expectations to the administrator
> ➤ Board members' use of authority and influence outside of meetings

5

THE WALK

BIG DOG KNEW it was time for a walk. Not just any walk, *the* walk. Duke, the school's Administrator, had been in his leadership position for a month and the stress was taking its toll on the proud canine. Duke hadn't said anything, but Big Dog's ability to read others was extraordinary. Through instinct and experience, he could tell by his friend's body language that Duke needed encouragement. Big Dog went by many names and not all of them were complimentary: Big Dog, Bernie, Hard Head, Big Goof, and others. But unmistakably, he had the gift of being able to understand others and respond in a sensitive way.

For the past few weeks, the slump in Duke's shoulders had increased each day. His jaws tightened often. His cool demeanor seemed a distant memory. Big Dog knew the importance of getting Duke out of his daily grind. His Administrator needed a change, even if for a little while today.

Duke looked up and Big Dog motioned to join him on the narrow path. While Duke bounded over, Big Dog guessed the shepherd would split from the path at the first opportunity when the pair entered the forest near the academy campus. Customary of his breed, Duke took a zigzag approach to explore the path while they walked. After a few minutes of chit-chat, Big Dog asked, "So how old were you when you learned to obey the Master?"

"That wasn't easy for me to learn." Duke slowed his pace. "Why do you ask?"

"I just want to get to know you a little better," Big Dog said.

"Will this be like another interview? But this time things about my childhood to determine why I am who I am? Stuff like that?"

Big Dog smiled.

"Well, if you must know." Duke surveyed the path and nearby bushes. "I started out under the care of an older couple who didn't really know what they were getting into with raising a hard-headed, rambunctious pup like me. Things didn't go well ...

"I recall the last evening I was there," he continued, "my owner's wife let him know that it was her or the dog." Big Dog noticed some wetness around his companion's eyes. "So the next thing I remember, I was staying at a new place with a lady and her two kids. They knew even less about raising a strong-willed teenager, so there was lots of yelling followed by long periods of being ignored. Their approach was to leave me out in the backyard where I was free to do my own thing as long as I didn't tear up anything. But I guess I wasn't taught about discipline or obedience in that situation either."

Big Dog listened intently and some of Duke's lack of trust with the Board members and his difficulty making relationships with some of the parents came into focus. His heart ached as the story unfolded and he regretted waiting until now to set aside time to talk.

Sadness slipped into Duke's voice as he continued. "Then one day a man and his wife came to visit me and asked the lady if I could come live with them. So I was moving again—my bed, my dish, my toys, everything were thrown into the back of a sports car and off I went. I recall thinking, 'If I could just live with someone who really loves me and takes the time to discipline me, I know I can do things the right way.'"

This gave Big Dog fresh insight to why and how Duke lovingly corrected some of the tougher students in the academy.

"For the first time I got to live indoors. But they had another dog there named Beau, another shepherd, who knew everything. Beau whispered in my ear that first afternoon, 'Relax. Just imitate me as I imitate the Master.'"

That apparently made all the difference.

"In the days that followed, I learned to control my urges, my impulsiveness, my energy. They taught me how to listen and obey. I really wanted to fit in and they helped me relax while living within the rules. For the first time in my life I was loved and they spent time with me. And my big brother in the house, well, he reminds me of you, except he was a lot smaller," Duke said, his lips curling in a grin. "In my companionship with Beau I experienced the friendship that I needed with a mature, complete leader. And he never let me down." Duke bounced into the underbrush to investigate a rustling.

Though this was supposed to be an opportunity for them to spend time together, Big Dog didn't feel offended because he knew the importance of Duke relaxing and having the opportunity to be himself. When Duke returned, Big Dog took the conversation in a new direction. "Let me make a guess here, based on what you have been telling me: when a Board member corners you about some problem in the academy or gives you the impression he is mad at you, your knee-jerk reaction is to pick up your water dish and move on to a new home?"

"I'm afraid that's spot on," Duke said. "It's tough for me to receive the criticism without thinking that I am going to be dismissed and sent packing."

"What do you think we can do about this? No dog should have to live that way."

Duke sniffed the path, perhaps considering his response. "You know what would really help me? If the council could tell me what they are looking for. You know, what they expect. And then tell me how they plan to measure whether or not I've actually completed the tasks."

Big Dog caught on quickly to where this was going. "And match this stuff to your job description that we gave you when you started. We could set this up and review things with you once every semester. How would that be?"

For the first time since their walk began, the pair came to a full stop. Duke looked squarely into the eyes of his mentor, a rare occurrence for his breed. "I appreciate you giving me this opportunity and I love the pups. I really do want to do my best and I trust you like no one since Beau. If we could work this job evaluation out, I think I would learn a lot. And I could relax and learn to trust the council and the process."

"Duke, we're going to make this happen. You and your water dish aren't going anywhere."

The walk ended moments later. Big Dog and Duke had returned to where they began today's venture. But not really. Things would never be the same. Big Dog had gained deep insight into how to serve the one he was called to lead. And it was evident that Duke had learned that trust frees one to be who the Master designed one to be.

DISCUSSION:

> What prompted the outing for the two dogs?
> What past experiences had an impact on Duke's ability to connect with others in the school community? Do adult leaders come to new situations as finished products?
> How important do you think it is to establish a close working relationship with an individual you are charged with the responsibility to oversee and evaluate? What is your understanding of the sentence in the last paragraph: "Big Dog had gained deep insight into how to serve the one he was called to lead"?
> What decision did the two come to agreement on? Has your board established such a process?

6

NEW COUNCIL MEMBERS

THE FIRST YEAR had been a howling success and the council gathered for the meeting in which three members would rotate off and the selection of three new members would take place.

Tonight the Board would say "good-bye" to Keta, the Husky, and Kelley, the Cocker Spaniel, who was the only remaining female from the original council. The Board had previously decided that each member would serve no longer than three years, with some of the original members rotating off with shorter terms so the three-year rotation could begin early in the academy's history. Also, it was established that Big Dog, as the original and current chairman, would be among the last to rotate off. After a year away, former council members would be eligible to return and serve another term.

They all agreed with the policy that was scribbled on the wall of their meeting place:

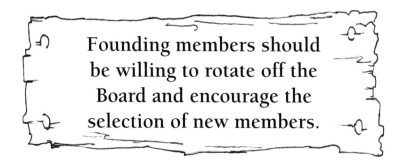

Founding members should be willing to rotate off the Board and encourage the selection of new members.

Rotating off after year one:
    Reneé, the French poodle
    Kelley, the Cocker Spaniel
    Keta, the Husky
Rotating off after year two:
    Corky, the mixed breed
    Sport, the large black dog
    Rusty, the brown Labrador Retriever
Rotating off after year three:
    Winston, the British Bull Dog
    Sage, the Shar Pei
    Big Dog, the Saint Bernard

Big Dog, Winston, and Sage, serving together as a subcommittee, had gathered the names of possible candidates from the council and identified three worthy of an interview. With no goal of replacing the outgoing female members with other females, the subcommittee introduced two females and one male:

    Samantha, a Great Dane
    Jackie, a Bouvier des Flandres

Maximilian, or Max, a Pug
Meg, a lovely Golden, was chosen as first alternate

Rejected was a regal Boxer named Remington. During the interview he had made it clear his preference was to develop a boarding school similar to Kennebunkport Kennels, where puppies were trained to compete in Kennel Club of America competitions.

Big Dog reviewed the interview process with the full council, including the key questions:

What is your relationship with your Master?
What is your view of the school's mission?
 What do you have to offer as a member of the council?

Each of the three candidates was invited to join the meeting, one at a time.

Max

Samantha, the Dane, was elegant, regal, and dignified. She flowed into the room with the longest legs Big Dog had ever seen. During the discussion, she admitted to sneaking treats off the kitchen counter. "Who could blame her," Sage quipped. "The food must be eye level for her!"

Thick hair covered the face and created a mysterious air about the next candidate, Jackie, the Bouvier des Flandres, a strong and athletic breed. The council was set at ease when they heard her gentle, thoughtful answers. "I think she'll be an excellent role model for young female pups," Winston said.

Max, the Pug, was affable and comfortable from the moment he rolled into the meeting room. He obviously struggled with controlling his weight, but no one on the current subcommittee was in a position to cast stones. "I believe he will help set an encouraging and positive esprit de corps among the council," Big Dog said.

All three candidates had the following qualities in common:

> Each was known for a submissive attitude towards his/her Master.
> Each had a reputation for loyalty and would be a strong supporter of the academy.
> Each was good with his/her own pups at home.

Samantha was put on a subcommittee to work with Duke on the policies regarding discipline procedures. Their goal was to guide the pups to grow in independence and self-discipline.

Jackie was assigned to review the academy's safety and security procedures. Duke had acknowledged that with a growing school, he could not be everywhere at once and his extraordinary senses of hearing and smell were stretched

Jackie

thin. More technical know-how in this area would support his training of the canine staff.

Max wasn't placed on a subcommittee right away. What went without saying was that he would not be involved with the lunch menus.

One last matter remained on the agenda this evening: the name of the academy. Big Dog reviewed the reason the school was established and thanked each dog for his/her role in the school's success. But what, he questioned, made their school distinctive from say, Pointer Prep or Mastiff Military School?

Sage spoke up first. "We are committed to seeing our pups grow to obey their Master."

Big Dog added, "Since we are all passionate to see this happen, let's change the name of our school from Canine Academy to something that reflects our mission more clearly."

Winston, in a rare moment of speaking in favor of change, suggested, "How about 'The Master's Academy'?"

And so it was confirmed—the school would have a name that declared the commitment and the intention of the council.

DISCUSSION:

> What was their plan for the election of new council members? Do you agree with the approach presented in this chapter? Why or why not?

> Do you have a prescribed process for interviewing and selecting new members? What questions do you think need to be asked of potential candidates?

> Some boards have the perspective, "Who is willing to serve?" What minimum expectations do you

believe are important as a standard for participation on your board?

➢ Why did the Canine Council change the name of the school?

7

SNOW DAY

BIG DOG WAS up before sunrise and wore a path in the yard in front of his house. He reviewed every step in the lesson plan he had meticulously crafted.

This was the day for which he had been waiting.

This was his day during which he would be "the sage on stage."

This was his day to be the presenter who would "wow" the young puppies.

He had waited weeks—for snow!

His nose flexed as he took in the weather change. He turned his face into the wind and relished the moist, crisp breeze. He watched the first flakes paint the neighborhood with white brush strokes. His tongue lapped at the huge crystals that promised a long day of snow and sizable accumulation. Big Dog closed his eyes and pulled in a deep breath. His heart accelerated as he reviewed the directions he would soon give the students. Without any pause to consider whatever needs his Master may have for the day, he hastened out to the street for a better view of the neighborhood.

Where were the students? Big Dog realized that in the haste to get The Master's Academy up and running, no plans were made for snow days. And apparently Duke had thought it best not to ring the bell that summoned the pups to school every day. In the absence of set policy or procedure, Duke, the school Administrator, must have concluded it was best to give students and teachers the day off.

Even though it was well past the normal start time, Big Dog called them in by ringing the cast iron bell that hung in the backyard. Unfortunately, a disappointing fifty percent of the students showed up. Worse yet, Duke trotted in with some of the last to arrive. Others may not have understood, but Big Dog knew this day could not be wasted—for any reason.

Big Dog paced and, in a louder than normal voice, discussed his plans for the morning with Duke. Many would miss out on the benefit of his personal experiences and expertise at tracking and rescuing animals and humans lost in the snow, skills the founder of the school considered vital for these young dogs as they approached adulthood. With a late start, valuable time had been lost and if the snow piled up too high, some of the students could become the object of a search themselves.

By the time the group set out, the snow had reached at least two inches. For some pups, this was up to their knees. The leaders were extra cautious as they herded the lively pack of pups through a vacant lot and into the forest that stretched the length of the northern border of the neighborhood.

The silence of the march was broken by Duke, who called from the rear of the pack. "How much farther? Some of us with soft pads have frost all over our paws!"

At the front, Big Dog stopped, spun, and raised a massive paw to halt the pack. He instructed everyone to gather around and barked out instructions about how to follow deer tracks left by a herd earlier that morning. Some of the older dogs shook their heads. How could they not understand? he thought. These commands are pretty simple.

Duke spoke up again. "Can we try sniffing out the immediate area before we begin tracking anyone so that we don't get confused?"

Big Dog knew this was a question from an inexperienced tracker and was yet another distraction. The deepening snow reminded Big Dog of numerous past rescues. He recounted a few in great detail, each time regaling in his hero's role. But some shuffling and throat clearing from the back of the circle encouraged Big Dog to cut the session short. He asked for a volunteer who would serve as the rescuee.

A young Husky jumped at the chance, but Duke spoke up. "I'll go and you guys can come find me."

Big Dog accepted the new volunteer's offer and asked the students to hide their eyes while their principal got a head start on the inexperienced search posse. With their faces covered by their tiny paws, Big Dog confronted Duke—again. He rose to his full height, his massive body towering over the unsuspecting Duke. Big Dog bared his teeth. "You don't get it, do you?"

"Get what?" Duke shot back, growling.

"I need to teach these pups how to track." Big Dog raised a paw. "And all you want to do is goof off. This is my school and I won't let the likes of you get in the way of today's lesson."

Giggling and yelping interrupted the confrontation. The youngest pups had stumbled upon a small, shallow stretch of frozen water, a natural ice rink created by the previous night's frigid temperature. They slid and glided across their new playground.

Duke clenched his jaw. Big Dog sensed his administrator wanted to laugh but wouldn't—couldn't—allow that during this important training. He glanced at the young pups and back at Duke, who shuddered.

"What's so funny?"

"Nothing," Duke replied through gritted teeth, his eyes belying his words.

A crescendo of laughter caught Big Dog's attention and he hustled to check on things. "Don't move," he called over his shoulder to Duke.

Wanting to take a closer look at this ice flow, he charged into the middle of the game and brushed away the newly fallen snow to learn more about the surface the kids played on. Some of the ice cracked and fell into the stream. Big Dog didn't panic. A little water wouldn't hurt anyone. In fact, the pups could learn a little about the properties of water. But they were behind schedule and the group must move on to the next step.

The sun peeked out from behind the clouds, hinting at the possibility that this special learning opportunity would soon be lost. Such a possibility heightened Big Dog's anxiety and he turned quickly on the slick surface.

Big Dog lost his footing and flopped face down into the water.

It was not supposed to turn out this way.

This was his lesson plan and it was supposed to be different.

And this was not how Big Dog had envisioned it.

As he pulled himself up, he caught a glimpse of his reflection in the pool of water, highlighted by a brief flash of sunlight. He barely recognized the face staring back at him. His facial muscles were taut, his eyes red with anger, his teeth clenched, and his jaw tight. *What have I become?* he wondered as passing clouds hid the sun and the image below him blurred. Was this the leader who had been called to lead a new generation of dogs who would mature and faithfully follow the Master?

He shivered and then shook, hoping to relax his taut muscles. He turned his attention back to the fun-loving pups who had all piled on Duke, covering him with fresh snow. It was obvious the pups loved their school leader and trusted him. He was exactly what the pups needed to point them toward obedience to the Master. Realizing the right lessons were being taught, Big Dog stood back for a moment before lumbering over and piling on top of Duke. After everyone was covered in snow, thoroughly soaking each other, Big Dog and Duke gathered the pups and led them back to the neighborhood.

When the last pup had been deposited home safely, Big Dog apologized for his behavior and invited Duke to his warm, overstuffed down pillow and for a bowl of warm milk. Today's lesson had not turned out anything like Big Dog had planned, but the day was a success.

DISCUSSION:

➤ What was Big Dog so excited about? Describe his emotions.

➤ What do you think the narrator means when he states on the first page of this chapter: "Without any pause to consider whatever needs his Master may have for the day"?

➤ Explain Duke's role in this chapter. Was he an effective administrator this particular day? Why or why not?

➤ What realization did Big Dog reach as his plans unraveled?

➤ In what areas of school life might a board member approach an event this way?

➤ How could you (a fellow board member) start a conversation if you saw this happening?

8

THE INTRUDER

DUKE SMELLED HIM before he saw him—Gus. No other dog smelled as bad. The poor little guy struggled with hygiene. Soon after he bathed, Gus would bolt right back into the mud, under a greasy car, or into a tight, dusty place. Notorious for eating anything he could, Gus's breath could peel paint off a wall. That wasn't the worst of it, though. The odors released from the other end made people want to vomit.

Truth be told, one good thing about Gus's problem was he could never sneak up on someone.

Duke heard the truck long before it appeared on the street in front of the academy. The shrill squeal of the brakes—unperceivable to some breeds and most humans—sounded in an adjacent neighborhood. Duke tilted his head and swiveled his ears. His muscular body flexed to full attention. He muttered a low whine.

Like others, Duke knew the appearance of this vehicle usually preceded the disappearance of a neighborhood pet. Duke thought, *Not today, not on my watch.* The school had a plan in place for such a situation, but he didn't want to sound the alarm too soon. A moment later the truck entered the neighborhood and Duke activated the emergency plan with three staccato barks.

The teachers sprang into action, just as they had practiced. The youngest pups followed their teacher into a narrow culvert, one too small for an adult man to enter. The middle set of pups dashed into a thicket of butterfly bushes. The oldest students bolted toward the neighbor's house and scooted through the doggy door in the garage, a convenient shelter that was locked during the day while the owner worked.

The truck screeched to a halt in front of the school. A burly man wearing hard-soled boots stepped onto the curb and surveyed the school. He tapped the end of a long stick on the sidewalk.

With everyone in place, Duke's job was to lead the intruder away from the academy yard. He barked three times and took off around the corner of the house. An overturned water dish, a broken limb, and two rocks stacked one on the other indicated all the students were safe. Duke waited on the opposite side of the driveway, near the front porch.

The intruder clomped around the corner and across the driveway past the garage door. Duke took off. When he reached the opposite side of the house, he activated the sprinkler system. The heads shot up from the ground like little soldiers ready to take care of business. And they did, soaking everything from one end of the house to the other and from the house to the front sidewalk.

The man glared at Duke and sloshed through the front yard. Surprisingly, he closed the gap quicker than Duke expected. When close enough, the man swung his oversized stick. Duke ducked, slipped around the corner, and set the next trap. He barked once and headed for the back corner.

The intruder rounded the corner and slammed into the ladder, spilling a can of yellow paint on his head. He wiped his eyes and pointed his stick at Duke. "Just wait till I get my hands on you."

Gus and his Teacher

Duke backed up, barked again, and ran to the middle of the backyard. He hadn't run like this in ages. Despite the circumstances, it felt good to run hard. He waited. Something wasn't right. Duke sniffed the air, but smelled only Gus. And the intruder must have as well.

Knowing a huddle of young dogs could not have tolerated being in a tight place with Gus, Duke had assigned him and a teacher to hide under the front porch, away from his classmates.

Duke retraced his steps, careful to not alert the intruder by stepping on an errant branch. He eased around the ladder and into the front yard. Duke spotted the man, on his hands and knees, crawling toward the secret hiding place. Duke sprung into action. With three quick jumps, he landed near the man, who was halfway under the porch. Duke bared his teeth above the man's ankle.

A shrill scream pierced the air.

Duke winced.

The man wiggled from underneath the porch, trying to push away an irate skunk.

Gus and the teacher bolted from underneath the porch, brushing past Duke while gasping for air.

Soaked with a heavy dose of skunk spray, the intruder bolted toward his truck. His words matched the stench emanating from his clothes.

When the man sped away, Duke signaled everyone return to the school. As the students and teachers returned in single file, Duke stood off to the side. Big Dog approached. His smile matched Duke's.

"Well done," said Big Dog.

"Just doing my job."

"You did it well. I hoped we'd never have to activate this plan, but it's nice to see that it works."

"It worked well. I'm—" Duke smelled him when he rounded the corner. Instead of holding his nose, Duke drew in a deep breath of Gus's odor, thankful that something bad can actually be turned around and used for something good.

DISCUSSION:

- ➢ What assignment had Duke received after his hiring?
- ➢ What role did the Board play in the development and execution of his plans?
- ➢ Do you have emergency plans established at your school?
- ➢ In what ways have they been communicated to those who are responsible for carrying them out?

9

THE AMBUSH

DUKE HAD A spring in his gait as he made his way down the path. The last few days had been successful ones for the pups. They were growing into their huge paws and he was hearing great reports about their obedience to their Master.

But he slowed when he entered the yard. His nostrils flared, his ears went up, his tail stiffened. Something was different, but Duke wasn't sure what. As he neared the Board's normal meeting place, Duke sensed others had been there and gone. Their scents were fresh so he must have just missed them. Did he have the incorrect time? Did he miss the meeting? The hair stood up on the back of his neck. His heart raced when he neared the door.

After calming himself, Duke stepped inside. Four dogs remained: Big Dog, the chairman of the council; Sage, the elder member of the council; Corky, the most affable member; and Winston, always the first to volunteer to attend any subcommittee meeting, especially if the agenda including parsing policies and procedures.

Though not threatened by the downcast appearance of the chairman, Duke's enthusiasm for the recent successes remained at the door as he entered slowly. His shoulders slumped. Something was amiss. The rest of the council had been dismissed or had chosen not to stick around for what was about to take place.

The ambush began.

The first jab—Kelley's pup had lost an expensive charm, a dazzling family heirloom. Her instructor had asked her to bring it for "show and tell." Against her better judgment, Kelley allowed her pup to take the jewel to school. The pup's fellow classmates "oohed" and "ahhhed" during the presentation. And soon after, it disappeared, slipping from the pup's neck during recess. The limited time invested in trying to find the jewelry upset Kelley.

The next punch—rabbits had invaded the school yard. Anything edible was gone. In its place were ragged foliage and disheveled mulch.

And the haymaker—plastic grocery bags, newspaper, and notebook paper blew across the yard like fallen leaves. The fresh coat of paint applied a few months ago had grown dingy, scattered paw prints appeared along the walls, and nose prints from dozens of curious pups peppered the windows.

Duke tried to defend himself, but was told to "pipe down."

And then someone finished unloading the gunny sack. Another parent's pup had accidentally lost his grip on his new balloon, and no one was available to scale the pine tree and retrieve it. The pup was inconsolable and the event disrupted their entire family, canines and humans alike. No one from the school apologized for the loss.

THE AMBUSH

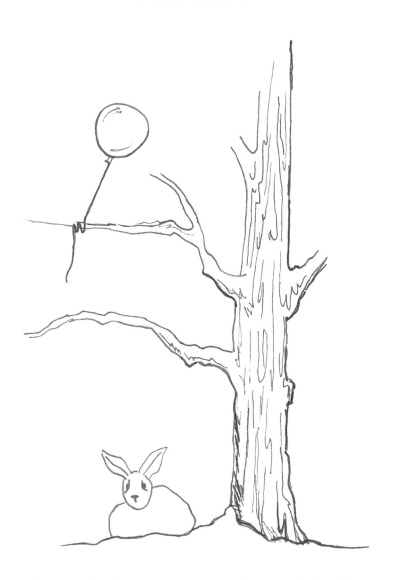

The assault of criticisms appeared over and the ad hoc disciplinary committee sat back on their haunches, apparently satisfied that they had vented their spleens sufficiently. Duke couldn't respond to the harsh drubbing. Finally, he said, "First, I'm disappointed that these reports were gathered behind my back without requiring these folks that I have upset to come to me, your chosen leader." He stared at the far wall. "If I may still call myself that." He pushed aside his hurt to continue. "May I point out that I did not misrepresent myself when you hired me two years ago. I did not present myself as having the nose of a Bloodhound with the capability to locate lost items. If you had wanted the fastidiousness of a French poodle, you selected the wrong canine. An adult my size can't climb trees, nor should he be expected to. If you wanted Mr. Meet and Greet, maybe a Lab would have served you better.

"I clearly remember that you described to me a list of qualifications and expectations that included me being a strong leader, a courageous pioneer, a brave protector of the pups of this community, and a creative problem solver for a growing school. I respectfully request that you evaluate my performance based on these standards as discussed when I was hired."

Duke hesitated for a moment, wondering if he should continue. He searched Big Dog's face for a reaction. When Duke saw none, he continued. "May I also ask why you met without me? Have I not always been respectful of your concerns and the needs of our parents and pups? Finding out that you felt the need to review school events and questions without me makes me think that you don't trust me to listen with an open mind to issues that impact our kids. That is very disappointing. I think I deserve better."

Big Dog lumbered over and placed his enormous nose next to Duke's. Silence hung heavy over the room until Big Dog broke the tension. "My brother, would you accept an apology from me on behalf of this Board? We meant well, but it is clear that we messed up in a number of areas that we need to correct. Can you stay for a while and help us work out how we can straighten out our procedures?"

The Board and Duke worked late, ignoring the rhythmic springtime chirping and singing. When they were finished hammering out the details, Big Dog posted three new procedures on the wall for ratification at the next full Board meeting.

To correct the gunny sacking of complaints about Duke:

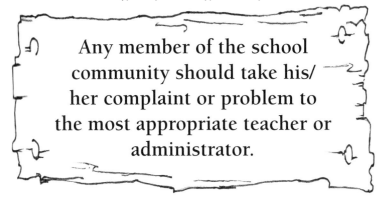

Any member of the school community should take his/ her complaint or problem to the most appropriate teacher or administrator.

To avoid wounding an Administrator by meeting without him, Big Dog led them in the creation of this new practice:

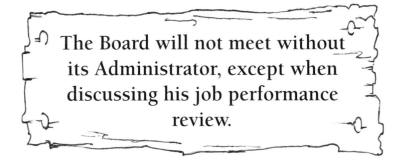

The Board will not meet without its Administrator, except when discussing his job performance review.

To further repair the loss of trust between the Board and Duke, the five agreed to establish a practice of measuring his performance based on his job description and—with his agreement—to create the methods for measurement in advance:

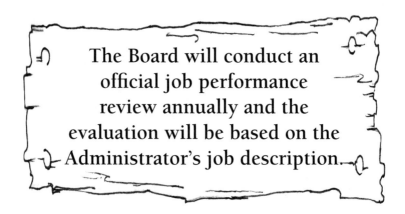

The Board will conduct an official job performance review annually and the evaluation will be based on the Administrator's job description.

Before leaving, each Board member took a turn at gnawing on an old bone, a symbolic gesture of forgiving and forgetting. Big Dog dug a suitable hole in the corner, tossed in the bone, and watched as each member helped cover it up.

DISCUSSION:

➤ What was the purpose of this gathering of Board members? How do you evaluate the charges brought against Duke? Are these illustrations unrealistic when you consider your school community?

➤ What do you think of the way the accusations were presented to Duke?

➤ Review Duke's responses to the criticisms. Were his answers appropriate or out-of-line?

➤ Discuss each of the three new procedures that were proposed. Do you have each of these in place? Why or why not?

THE AMBUSH

➤ Is it possible to make the specific requirements in the job performance measurable? Give an example that fits your current situation.

10

LOST AND FOUND

MAYBE THE SAME spring weather that had affected the pups so much now energized the older canines. Maybe gathering for the final meeting of the school year and finishing on a high note created the electricity that Big Dog felt.

Or maybe it was because Duke was bringing along a special guest.

Whatever the reason, Big Dog observed a liveliness and bounce to the group he had not noticed before. Canines aren't supposed to be able to anticipate the future, but they felt like something extraordinary was about to take place at their meeting.

As each dog settled into his or her usual space in Big Dog's home, Duke, the Administrator of the Master's Academy, entered with a dog of equal size at his side. Tonight's main agenda item was the opportunity for the Board to interact with the candidate Duke had selected to become the school's Assistant Administrator.

Several events and key decisions had led up to this moment. Early on some members of the newly elected Canine Council had felt it their responsibility to know about and put their paw print on nearly every decision Duke made. But as Duke earned everyone's trust and the Board got better at establishing boundaries of authority, Big Dog convinced them of the wisdom of having a more "paws off" approach to the daily running of the academy.

This way of thinking had led to the significant decision for the Board not to interview every potential teacher, but to hold Duke responsible for selecting his staff. Big Dog pointed to the statement on the wall as a reminder of what had previously been agreed to.

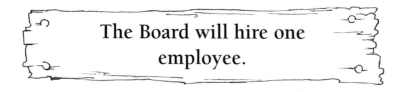

The Board will hire one employee.

The Board's subcommittees, like the finance committee and curriculum committee, were functioning in a positive way to provide direction for major areas of the school. But the group had removed itself entirely from the significant task of hiring and firing. All agreed, Duke was doing a marvelous job of keeping them informed of these significant decisions.

Because this was his first hire for the academy's leadership team, the Board had instructed Duke to give them a chance to meet and interact with his choice before the final decision was made. This Board had agreed at an earlier meeting to create the position of assistant head of school. Duke won their support for the idea by providing information about his workload, his health (bloodshot eyes and clumps of fur falling out), and the school's growing enrollment, accelerated by students transferring from Pointer Prep.

Big Dog had not been introduced to the dog at Duke's side, but he felt like he knew him. Duke had shared with Big Dog the great qualities of this candidate, especially those characteristics that complemented his. This younger dog would be a real help to Duke and the growing academy.

Big Dog's nose reflexively rose as the stranger entered and sat in the center with Duke. His nostrils flared as what he thought were familiar scents tickled his olfactory memory. Perhaps the two had met before. Big Dog dismissed the notion as confusion with the memory of another dog.

With a nod from Big Dog, Duke cleared his throat and began to speak. "Thanks for being here tonight to meet the individual whom I hope will become my assistant. As we discussed at a previous meeting, I was to interview candidates for this new position and introduce you to the one that I believe to be best qualified."

Big Dog could not help but notice how much Duke's leadership and influence had grown in such a short time. It had not always been evident. But then again, Bernie and the other Board members had grown along with him.

Yes, Duke's demeanor and poise in Board meetings had grown with his increased awareness of his responsibilities, but tonight was special. He exuded a confidence that was remarkable. It seemed Duke knew something that the others didn't. Big Dog wondered if anyone else sensed this as well. He crossed his front paws while taking in the inspiring style of the academy's leader.

Duke continued, "Tonight it's my pleasure to introduce you to Banderos, an experienced educator that embraces our school's mission—to train students to serve the Master. I thought we would take a few moments to let him tell you his story."

With quick, fluid movement, the new dog sprang up on cue. Big Dog felt pity for the dog's teachers. They must have had their hands full with this one, he thought. He guessed the dog's breed to be a Walker, similar to a Blue Tick Hound. Powerful, athletic, and quicker than all the Board members, no pup at the school could get one over on this guy. He spoke with a clear and steady voice.

"I have heard about what is happening here in your community and would be honored to become a part of your academy. With my training and experience, I believe that I am qualified to be Duke's assistant and to learn from him about leading a school. And as he just said, I believe strongly in training pups to listen to and obey the Master." He paused while the Board members eyed him carefully.

Sage asked an insightful question. "What do you believe is your strength or best quality that you bring to our school?"

Banderos shifted his weight from one leg to the other. He glanced at Duke, who smiled. "May I call you Sage? That is your name, right?" When Sage nodded, Banderos continued. "My strength is also my weakness. I believe I can effectively teach and lead your pups to learn to obey the Master because I have not always done so."

The handsome dog paused and squared his shoulders. "You see, I have not always been obedient and disciplined. Some in this room may remember me by my nickname: 'Bandit.'"

Big Dog sprang from his prone posture and barked, "I knew it! I knew it! I knew there was something familiar about you!" He ran and smothered his friend with the huge hug only a Saint Bernard can give. After several minutes, Big Dog, choking back tears, blurted in rapid-fire a few questions: "I thought you were … How did you … When did you …?"

Banderos

The other Board members had gathered round the prodigal pup. What formality that had existed was lost for good.

When Big Dog let go, Bandit regained his footing and his breath. "The night I disappeared was the turning point. I got lost and wandered out to the highway where I was hit by a car and left for dead in a ditch until morning. One of the last things I remember was Big Dog calling out to me."

"So what happened?" Sage urged him to continue.

"An amazing man named Sam found me along the highway and took me to the vet. He paid my medical bills. But because I had taken my collar off, he had no idea where I was from. He brought me home to live with him.

"For the first time, I experienced consistent, loving discipline. Sam taught me to control myself and be obedient. And now I am ready to train others."

The meeting ended soon after, a record for this group, but the members had much to celebrate! Of course, Banderos was approved and invited to begin immediately, if Sam approved.

When Big Dog finally lay down for the night, he rested peacefully knowing his dream had become reality: Pups were being rescued, even Bandit, and they were being trained to follow the Master.

DISCUSSION:

➢ How has the Board's relationship with Duke changed? Can you give examples from the story that contributed to this change?

➢ To what extent does your own board agree with and practice the approach adopted by the story's Board— that you as the board hire only one employee?

➤ Has the relationship between the Board chairman and the academy's Administrator changed? In what way?

➤ What were the reasons for adding an Assistant Administrator? Do similar conditions exist at your school?

Summary of the Board procedures of the Master's Academy:

The mission/vision of the school should be clearly understood by all the leaders.

Board members should evaluate one employee: the Administrator. The boundaries of his authority and the Board's expectations should be clearly articulated.

Board members have authority only when they are involved in an officially called meeting and should not interject themselves into the daily affairs of the school.

The Board should develop a close working relationship with the Administrator.

Founding members should be willing to rotate off the Board and encourage the selection of new members.

Each Board member should contribute by giving financially and through their personal interests and abilities.

The Board should insure the protection of the ethical, financial, legal, and physical security of the school, including the safety of the students.

Board members should direct community members who have criticism to the appropriate administrator or staff member.

The Board should include the Administrator in all meetings except for the time of his/her evaluation.

The Board will conduct an official job performance review annually, and the evaluation will be based on the Administrator's job description.

What Dogs Can't Do
Suggested Bible studies with your board: